LIFE
SCIENCE
STORIES

Life in Extreme Places

Leon Gray

raintree
a Capstone company — publishers for children

Raintree is an imprint of Capstone Global Library Limited, a company incorporated in England and Wales having its registered office at 264 Banbury Road, Oxford OX2 7DY – Registered company number: 6695582

www.raintree.co.uk
myorders@raintree.co.uk

Text © Capstone Global Library Limited 2016
The moral rights of the proprietor have been asserted.

Produced for Raintree by Calcium
Edited by Sarah Eason and Harriet McGregor
Designed by Paul Myerscough and Geoff Ward
Picture research by Rachel Blount
Production by Victoria Fitzgerald
Originated by Capstone Global Library Limited © 2016
Printed and bound in China

ISBN 978 1 4747 1576 8 (hardback)
19 18 17 16 15
10 9 8 7 6 5 4 3 2 1

ISBN 978 1 4747 1582 9 (paperback)
20 19 18 17 16
10 9 8 7 6 5 4 3 2 1

British Library Cataloguing in Publication
A full catalogue record for this book is available
from the British Library.

Acknowledgements
We would like to thank the following for permission to reproduce photographs: Dreamstime: Cappui 27, Karin59 26; NOAA 8, 9; Science Photo Library: Solvin Zankl/ Visuals Unlimited 6; Shutterstock: Andreas Altenburger 22, Daniel Alvarez 17, Can Balcioglu 21, Hagit Berkovich 10, Ryan M. Bolton 16, ChameleonsEye 4, EastVillage Images 20, Eder 14, Gentoo Multimedia Ltd 13, Gertjan Hooijer 15, Matt Jeppson 18, D. Kucharski & K. Kucharska 28, 29, Ivan Kuzmin 19, Chris Lishman 23, Vladimir Melnik 12, PavelSvoboda 25, Prapat1120 24, SLLTH 5, Igor Stepovik 7, Synchronista 11.

Cover photographs reproduced with permission of: Shutterstock: Gentoo Multimedia Ltd.

Every effort has been made to contact copyright holders of material reproduced in this book. Any omissions will be rectified in subsequent printings if notice is given to the publisher.

Some words are shown in bold, **like this**. You can find out what they mean by looking in the glossary.

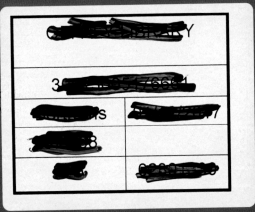

Contents

Extreme Earth

Imagine living in a place so incredibly hot that you could fry an egg in the heat of the sun. How would you stay cool? Think about what it would be like to live at the bottom of the sea. How would you survive in complete darkness, with the enormous weight of the water above pushing down on you?

Changing to survive

Many animals and plants have made their homes in some of Earth's most extreme places. Over time, they have changed to survive in these tough zones. This slow, gradual change is called **adaptation**.

The Namib beetle lives in the hot, dry desert of south-western Africa. It survives by drinking water from fog in the air.

DEEP FREEZE

The North and South Poles are freezing cold places at the far north and south of our planet. They are so cold that few plants can grow there. Only animals that do not eat plants, such as seals, penguins and polar bears, can live in these icy lands.

The North and South Poles are covered by a thick layer of snow and ice for most of the year.

Deep water

It is difficult to live in the deep ocean. The water is very cold and the weight of it pushes down from above. Sunlight cannot reach the deep waters, so it is completely dark. Deep-sea fish and other animals cannot see to find their way around. Instead, they use senses such as touch, smell and hearing to move around in the darkness.

Finding food

Plants cannot grow in the deep ocean because they need sunlight to make their own food. Some deep-sea animals feed on other deep-sea animals. Others eat dead plants and animals that sink down to the bottom of the ocean.

This hatchetfish lights up its body to draw in **prey**, frighten **predators** and "talk" to other hatchetfish.

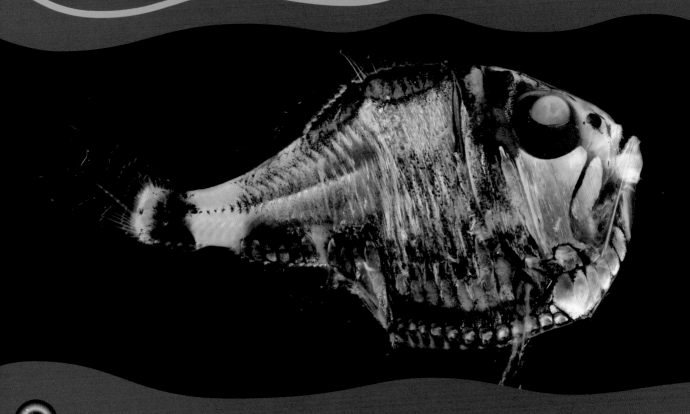

LIGHT SHOW

Some deep-sea animals make chemicals in their bodies that glow in the dark. Food is hard to find in the deep ocean so many deep-sea animals, such as jellyfish, glow to attract prey.

The **tentacles** of these jellyfish are covered with stinging **cells**. The cells inject poison into prey to kill it.

Bottom of the sea

When cold seawater trickles through cracks on the ocean floor, **hydrothermal vents** are created inside the Earth. Hot, molten rock heats the seawater. The boiling water then shoots out through the cracks in the ocean floor.

Living on the edge

Amazingly, a group of tiny creatures live in the boiling water near hydrothermal vents. They are called **extremophiles** because they live in such an extreme place. The extremophiles feed on the chemicals in the water. Larger creatures including giant clams, limpets and 2.5-metre- (8-feet-) long tube worms survive by eating the extremophiles.

Sea anemones cling on to the rocks near hydrothermal vents. They eat some of the animals that feed on the extremophiles.

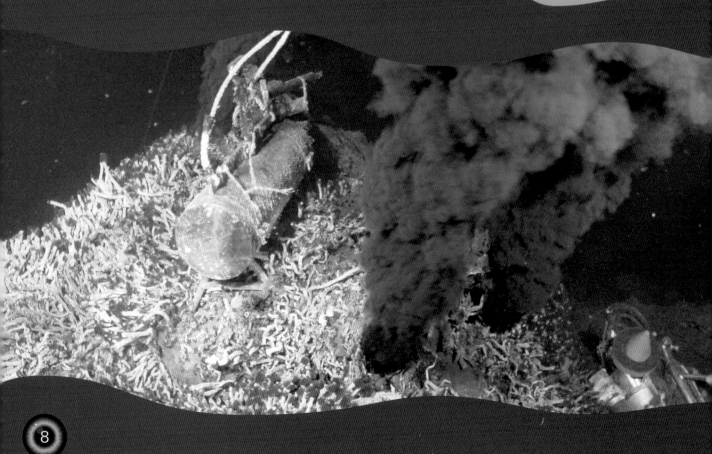

DEEP-SEA WORMS

Tube worms are always one of the first animals to appear near a new hydrothermal vent. Baby tube worms, called **larvae**, can swim. They cling on to rocks near the vent and grow into adults. As adults, they stay on the vent for the rest of their lives.

Extremophiles live inside the bodies of these tube worms. The extremophiles make food from chemicals in the water, and the tube worms then eat the food.

Desert heat

Deserts are extreme places because they are so hot and dry. The world's biggest desert is the Sahara in Africa. The temperature can reach 50 degrees Celsius (122 degrees Fahrenheit) and it hardly ever rains.

Life in the desert

Plants and animals have adapted to keep cool and save water in the dry desert. To survive, some plants have short roots that soak up water on the ground when it rains. Others have long roots that find water deep underground. Many animals only come out at night or live underground to hide away from the sun.

The big ears of the fennec fox have an important job to do. The fox loses body heat through its ears to keep cool.

SAVING WATER

A plant called a cactus can survive without rainwater for a long time. Some cacti store water in their stems. The stems swell up with water when it rains and the cacti then use the stored water when it is dry. Cacti also have waxy skin to stop water from leaking out.

The Saguaro cactus lives in the deserts of the southern United States and Mexico. The stem of the cactus can store huge amounts of water.

Freezing Poles

The polar lands are the Arctic in the far north of the planet and Antarctica in the far south. These places are so cold that it hardly rains there, so it is very dry. For many months of the year, it is also dark all day.

The Arctic and Antarctica

A thick layer of ice and snow covers Antarctica. There are no trees or shrubs there – only simple plants, such as mosses, grow. Most animals, such as seals and penguins, live in the surrounding oceans. Although the Arctic is just as tough to live in, more wildlife live there, from lichens and mosses to Arctic hares and polar bears.

This baby seal has a thick layer of blubber and waterproof fur to keep it warm in the freezing polar waters.

The Emperor penguin is the world's largest penguin. The bird has a large, round body and a lot of thick feathers to keep it warm.

Survival story

CUDDLING UP

The Emperor penguin is the only animal that lives in Antarctica during the tough winter. The birds breed in the winter, and the females leave the males on the ice to look after the eggs. The males cuddle up to keep warm in the icy winds.

Mountain high

Mountains cover 20 per cent of Earth's surface. The highest mountain on land is Mount Everest. It is 8 kilometres (5 miles) high. There are even bigger mountains under the sea. The island of Hawaii is the top of a huge mountain in the Pacific Ocean.

Tough living

Forests cover the lower slopes of a mountain. Many animals live in the trees or eat parts of them. Life is tougher higher up the slopes. Trees and plants die out to leave just bare rock covered in snow and ice. The air is thin, so there is less **oxygen** for animals to breathe. It is very cold, and animals need thick fur to keep warm.

These flowers are growing in a meadow on the lower slopes of a mountain.

MOUNTAIN MOVER

The ibex is a type of goat. It lives in the Alps, in Europe. The ibex is an amazing climber. It has a large heart and lungs that can take in a lot of oxygen from the thin air. It also has a very thick coat of fur to keep its body warm.

The ibex has hooves that grip on to rocks so that it can climb steep mountain slopes.

Faraway islands

Islands are areas of land that are surrounded by the sea. Although islands are separated from the mainland, animals and plants have still found their way there.

Island life

Most life is carried to islands either by the wind or by ocean **currents**. Some plant seeds float and then wash up on the seashore. Other seeds are light and are blown in the wind. Strong winds pick up tiny insects and spiders and carry them to islands. Some birds fly long distances and **roost** on islands. They drop seeds from their feathers and in their waste. Other animals drift on logs and then land on islands.

These tortoises live on the Galápagos Islands in the Pacific Ocean. The very first tortoises travelled to the islands by floating on ocean currents.

DARWIN'S FINCHES

Birds called finches live on the Galápagos Islands. They flew there from South America. Over time, the finches grew different beak shapes to eat different foods. The **biologist** Charles Darwin collected some of the finches when he visited the islands. They helped Darwin to come up with his idea that animals adapt, or **evolve**, in order to survive.

This Galápagos finch has a thin, sharp beak and eats insects and grubs. Other finches have large, thick beaks and eat nuts and seeds.

Underground caves

Caves are dark, damp places. Plants do not grow there because there is no sunlight or soil. Some plants, such as ferns, grow at the entrances to caves. The roots of other plants grow down through the roofs of caves.

What's for dinner?

Without plants to eat, cave animals must survive by finding different foods to eat. Some animals eat dead leaves that wash into the caves when it rains. Others eat **bacteria**, which live on the surface of rocks and in cave water. Some even eat the waste that bats and salamanders leave behind. Life inside a cave is hard!

The cave salamander is blind. It uses smell and touch to find its way around the cave.

THE BAT CAVE

Bats are the only mammals that live in caves. Millions of bats live in some caves. Bats hang upside down from the roof of the cave to sleep during the day. At night, the bats leave the cave to hunt small insects in the dark.

Bats are blind so they use their amazing sense of hearing to find their way around.

Hot water

Hot springs are pools of water that have been heated by hot rocks inside Earth. Most hot springs are about 38 degrees Celsius (100 degrees Fahrenheit). Some are so hot that they could burn you. The hot water contains minerals. The minerals sometimes turn the water into an acid, which can also burn skin.

Life in the pool

Hot springs are extreme places in which to live, but **bacteria** can survive in the boiling water. Bacteria at the surface of the spring make food by using the energy from sunlight. Bacteria below the surface feed on the minerals in the water.

Bacteria in this hot spring in Yellowstone National Park, in the United States, give the water its bright colours.

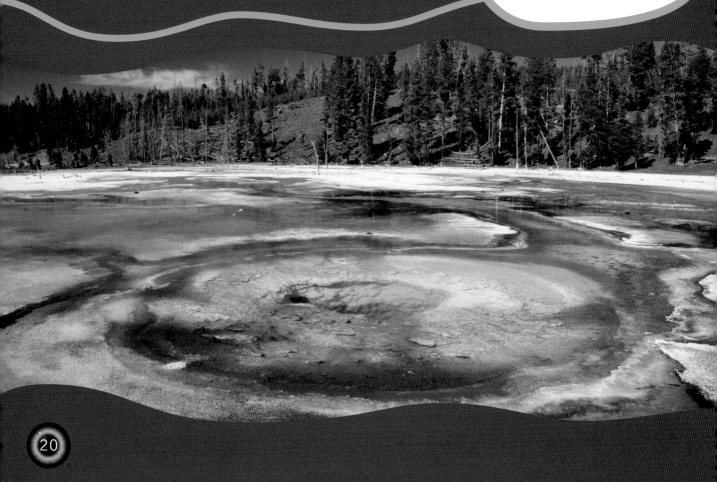

TIME FOR A BATH

One group of monkeys named Japanese macaques live in the mountains of Honshu – the main island of Japan. Snow falls for many months of the year there, and it is freezing cold. The monkeys bathe in hot springs to keep warm.

Macaques love bathing in the warm water of hot springs. There, they **groom** one another.

On the rocks

Rock pools form because of **tides**. At high tide, waves crash onto the rocky seashore and cold, salty seawater fills holes in the rocks. Sea animals hide in the holes to escape the waves. When the sea goes out at low tide, the animals in the holes are cut off from the ocean, and must survive in the rock pool.

Life in the pool

Rock pool life is tough, but many animals can still survive in them. Shellfish, such as mussels, often live in shallow rock pools. Sea anemones, starfish and small fish are usually found in deeper pools that are closer to the sea.

Crabs often become trapped in deep rock pools. They then feed on tiny animals in the seawater and seaweed that covers the rocks.

HOLD ON TIGHT

There is a lot of seaweed along the seashore near rock pools. The seaweed sticks to the rocks using a root-like part called a holdfast. Although seaweed looks like a plant and makes food from sunlight in the same way as a plant, it is not a true plant.

Seaweed covers rocks along the shore. It is an important food for many sea animals.

On the edge

Some animals live on a knife-edge – the rocky ledge of a cliff. Seabirds often lay their eggs on these narrow ledges. The nests of thousands of seabirds can stretch across a cliff. The birds live in a cramped space with salty sea spray and strong winds, but here they are safe from any **predators**.

Bottom of the cliff

Some animals and plants can survive the pounding waves at the bottom of the cliff. Seaweed clings to rocks here. **Invertebrates**, such as limpets, grip the rocks using their strong feet.

Mussels hook a tough, hairy thread into the rock face to hang on to rocks at the bottom of cliffs.

Survival story

CLIFFTOP HOME

Puffins are colourful seabirds that build nests on clifftops. Some puffins dig burrows in the soil. Others nest in cracks in the rocky cliffs. The puffins fly out to sea to catch fish and return to their nests to feed their young.

Puffins have waterproof feathers to protect them from cold winds. Their webbed feet help them them to swim in the sea.

Bogs and swamps

Bogs and swamps are called **wetlands** because the ground is soaked with water. Bogs are found in rainy places. They are spongy, mossy wetlands where plants grow faster than they **rot** away. Swamps are similar to bogs, but water from rivers or the sea floods the land. Trees are the main plants that grow in swamps.

Animal life

Wetland animals have adapted to life in water. Some animals live in the water and are good swimmers. Many wetland birds have long legs to stand clear of the water and hunt fish. Tiny insects, such as pond skaters, float on the water.

This beaver will spend most of its life in water. It has webbed feet and a wide tail to help it swim. Waterproof fur helps the animal to stay dry.

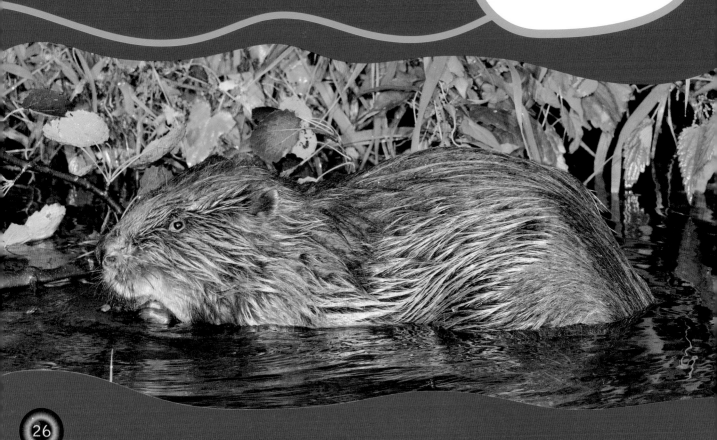

LIFE IN THE SWAMPS

Mangrove swamps form along coasts where salty seawater washes into rivers. Mangrove trees are the main plants in these swamps. Many different animals live in mangrove swamps, such as crabs, sea snakes and saltwater crocodiles.

The roots of these mangrove trees stand above the water. They grow down deep into the mud so the **tides** do not wash the trees away.

Life inside you

Some tiny creatures live inside the bodies of other animals – including humans. **Bacteria** are so small that they can only be seen under a microscope. Some bacteria are helpful, such as the bacteria in our gut, which help to break down food. Other bacteria are harmful and cause diseases that make us ill.

A living home

The human body can also be a home for tiny animals called **parasites**. Some live inside our bodies and feed on the food we eat. Others live on the outside of our bodies. Like many living things, they have adapted to survive in one of the most extreme places on Earth – our bodies!

Tiny insects called head lice can live in our hair. They use their sharp mouthparts to bite through our skin and drink our blood.

GUT FEELING

Tapeworms live inside the guts of people and other animals, who are known as their "host". They have a never-ending supply of food in the gut, so they can grow to be incredibly long – up to 10 metres (33 feet) long! The worms fold up their long bodies to fit inside the gut.

The tapeworm uses these tiny hooks on its head to grab on to the wall of the gut. This stops the worm from passing out of the animal host in its waste.